Your Magic Journal

This journal belongs to:

_____

Belffy Cat

Daily Gratitude and Manifestation Companion for A Better Life

"Whoever has _gratitude_ will be given more, and he or she will have an abundance. Whoever does not have _gratitude_, even what he or she has will be taken from him or her."

— Rhonda Byrne, The Magic

28 Days of Magical Practices to Transform Negative Situations and Cultivate Gratitude and Happiness.

Revolutionize Your Health, Money, Job, and Relationships, and Make Your Desires and Dreams a Reality.

INTRODUCTION TO YOUR MAGIC JOURNAL

Welcome to Your Magic Journal! This journal is designed to be a companion to The Magic Book by Rhonda Byrne, and it is designed to help you transform your life through the power of gratitude and manifestation. This journal is the perfect place for you to document your journey and celebrate your progress as you make gratitude a new habit and completely transform your life.

Gratitude and manifestation are two powerful tools that can help you attract abundance, happiness, and success into your life. By focusing on the things you are grateful for and actively visualizing the life you want to create, you can tap into the power of the universe and bring your desires to fruition.

Your Magic Journal is designed to be a place for you to reflect on your daily gratitude practices, record your goals and desires, and track your progress as you manifest the life of your dreams. Each page provides space for you to document your daily gratitude practices, and there is also space for you to write your goals and desires, as well as record your thoughts and reflections on your journey.

We have also included daily inspiring quotes to encourage and motivate you on your journey. These quotes have been carefully selected to help you stay focused and positive, and they serve as a reminder of the power that lies within you. Additionally, we have included examples of affirmations and visualization exercises to help you manifest your desires more effectively. Affirmations are positive statements that you repeat to yourself, and they can help you change your thought patterns and create a more positive outlook on life. Visualization exercises, on the other hand, help you bring your desires to life by imagining them as though they have already happened.

So, let's get started on this magical journey! By making gratitude a new habit and harnessing the power of manifestation, you can transform your life in amazing ways. This journal is here to help you along the way, so make use of it, be honest with yourself, and allow yourself to be amazed at the magic that unfolds before you. Make every day count and never give up on your dreams and desires. With determination and a positive attitude, you will reach your goals and create the life of your dreams.

ADDITIONAL RESOURCES FOR PRACTICING GRATITUDE

In addition to the principles outlined in "The Magic" by Rhonda Byrne, there are many other resources available to help you cultivate a daily practice of gratitude. Here are some tips and suggestions to help you get started:

Practice mindfulness: It is an effective way to cultivate gratitude and improve your overall well-being. Mindfulness involves being present in the moment and paying attention to your thoughts, feelings, and physical sensations. It's a way of training your mind to be more focused and aware, and it can help you feel more connected to the world around you.

Here are some tips for practicing mindfulness:
1. Find a quiet space: Find a quiet and comfortable place where you can sit or lie down without distractions. Turn off your phone and other devices, and close your eyes if you like.
2. Focus on your breath: Begin by taking a few deep breaths, inhaling deeply through your nose, and exhaling slowly through your mouth. Focus your attention on your breath, and try to stay focused on the sensation of the air entering and leaving your body.
3. Notice your thoughts: As you focus on your breath, you may find that your mind starts to wander. When this happens, simply notice your thoughts and bring your attention back to your breath. Don't try to suppress your thoughts, just observe them and let them pass by.
4. Stay in the moment: Try to stay focused on the present moment, and don't worry about the past or future. If your mind starts to wander, simply bring your attention back to your breath.
5. Practice regularly: Make mindfulness a daily habit, and try to practice for at least 10-15 minutes each day. You can also try incorporating mindfulness into your daily routine, such as during your morning coffee or while you're waiting in line.
6. Be patient: Mindfulness takes practice, and it can be challenging to stay focused at first. Be patient with yourself, and don't get discouraged if your mind wanders. Over time, you'll find that it becomes easier to stay focused and be present in the moment.

Incorporating mindfulness into your daily routine can help you feel more centered and focused, and it can also help you cultivate gratitude by increasing your awareness of the present moment and the blessings in your life. Whether you're just starting out or you're looking to deepen your practice, mindfulness can be a valuable tool for cultivating gratitude and improving your overall well-being.

Give back to others: *Helping others can bring a sense of fulfillment and gratitude to your life. Whether it's volunteering your time, donating to a charity, or simply being there for a friend, giving back can help you feel more connected to others and the world around you. Consider finding ways to give back that align with your values and interests, and make it a regular part of your routine.*

Engage in physical activity: *Exercise and physical activity can help release endorphins and improve your mood, making it easier to focus on what you're grateful for. Whether it's a daily yoga practice, a brisk walk in nature, or a high-intensity workout, find an activity that you enjoy and make it a regular part of your routine.*

Practice affirmations: *Repeating positive affirmations each day can help you focus on what you're grateful for and reinforce a positive outlook. Write down affirmations that resonate with you, and repeat them to yourself each day. You can also use visualization techniques to imagine yourself living a life filled with gratitude and abundance. You will find more resources on this topic later in this journal.*

Take time for self-care: *Taking care of yourself, whether it's through exercise, meditation, or simply taking a relaxing bath, can help you feel refreshed and rejuvenated, making it easier to focus on what you're grateful for. Make self-care a priority in your life, and find ways to treat yourself with kindness and compassion.*

Practice gratitude in difficult times: *It can be especially challenging to cultivate gratitude during difficult times, but it is precisely during these times that gratitude can be most transformative. When faced with adversity, try to focus on what you're grateful for, even if it's just one small thing. This can help you maintain a positive perspective and find hope in even the most trying of circumstances.*

Celebrate your blessings: *Take time each day to celebrate the blessings in your life. Whether it's expressing gratitude for a warm meal, a comfortable bed, or a beautiful day, take a moment to acknowledge and appreciate the good things in your life. You can also celebrate your blessings with others by sharing what you're grateful for and encouraging others to do the same.*

Remember, the key to cultivating gratitude is to make it a daily habit. By incorporating these additional resources into your life, you can deepen your practice of gratitude and experience the many benefits it brings. Whether you're just starting out or looking to take your gratitude practice to the next level, these tips and resources can help you cultivate an attitude of gratitude and live a more fulfilling life.

THE POWER OF WRITING YOUR GOALS: A KEY ELEMENT IN THE MAGIC PROCESS

Writing your goals is a critical step in the "magic" process as it sets the foundation for manifestation and attracts positive changes into your life. It helps you focus your thoughts and energy on what you truly want, making it more likely that you will attain it. In this part, we will explore the many benefits of writing your goals and why it is an essential part of the magic process.

When you write down your goals, you are making a commitment to yourself to achieve them. This act of committing to your goals increases your motivation and drive, as you can see them in front of you every day, reminding you of what you are working towards. By putting your desires into a concrete form, you can also better visualize what you want, making it easier to attract it into your life.

In addition to increasing motivation, writing your goals also helps you prioritize what is important to you. When you see your goals in writing, you can determine which ones are the most pressing and allocate your time and energy accordingly. This helps you focus on what is truly important to you and make intentional choices that will lead you closer to your desired outcome.

Moreover, writing your goals helps you overcome self-doubt and negative thinking. When you see your goals written down, it makes them seem more tangible and attainable, even if they may seem far-fetched at first. This can help you overcome any self-doubt or negative thoughts that may arise and keep you focused on what you want to achieve.

Another benefit of writing your goals is that it creates accountability. When you write down your goals, you are holding yourself accountable for making them a reality. This can help you stay motivated and focused, as you are no longer just thinking about your goals, but actively working towards them.

In conclusion, writing your goals is a key element in the magic process as it sets the foundation for manifestation and attracts positive changes into your life. It helps you focus your thoughts and energy, increase motivation, prioritize what is important, overcome self-doubt and negative thinking, create accountability, and ultimately lead you closer to your desired outcome. So, take the time to write down your goals and see the magic unfold.

MY GOALS/DREAMS FOR THE NEXT 28 DAYS:

1. _____

2. _____

3. _____

4. _____

5. _____

6. _____

7. _____

8. _____

9. _____

10. _____

" It's important to set your own goals and work hard to achie e them."

- YUICHIRO MIURA

MY GOALS/DREAMS FOR THIS YEAR:

1. _____

2. _____

3. _____

4. _____

5. _____

6. _____

7. _____

8. _____

9. _____

10. _____

"Those who don't believe in magic will never find it."

— ROALD DAHL

My Health and Body Goals:

1. _____

2. _____

3. _____

4. _____

5. _____

My Career and Work Goals:

1. _____

2. _____

3. _____

4. _____

5. _____

My Financial and Money Goals:

1. _____

2. _____

3. _____

4. _____

5. _____

My Relationships Goals:

1. _____

2. _____

3. _____

4. _____

5. _____

My Personal Desires:

1. _____

2. _____

3. _____

4. _____

5. _____
_____

My Material Desires:

1. _____

2. _____

3. _____

4. _____

5. _____
_____

MAKE GRATITUDE YOUR NEW HABIT AND COMPLETELY TRANSFORM YOUR LIFE!

Marking off every day in your gratitude journal not only helps you keep track of your progress, but it also serves as a visual reminder of the good things in your life. It creates a sense of accomplishment and encourages you to continue making gratitude a daily habit. By doing this, you not only train your brain to focus on the positive, but you also increase your overall happiness and satisfaction in life.

Transform your life by making gratitude your new habit and marking off each day in your journal.

Celebrate your progress and watch as your life becomes filled with joy and positivity.

Week 1	1	2	3	4	5	6	7	1
Week 2	8	9	10	11	12	13	14	2
Week 3	15	16	17	18	19	20	21	3
Week 4	22	23	24	25	26	27	28	4

"When I started counting my blessings, my whole life turned around."

- Willie Nelson

Magic Gratitude Subjects:

1. Health and Body

2. Work and Success

3. Money

4. Relationships

5. Passions

6. Happiness

7. Love

8. Life

9. Nature: Planet Earth. Air. Water. And the Sun

10. Material Goods and Services

11. Any Subject of Your Choosing

The Magic Gratitude Subjects are categories or areas in your life that you can express gratitude for in your journal. These can range from your health, relationships, job, financial situation, home, and others. By focusing on these subjects and writing down what you are grateful for, you can cultivate a positive mindset and attract abundance and happiness into your life. This structured gratitude practice can enhance the benefits of the Law of Attraction.

DAY 1   Date: _____

TODAY, I AM TRULY GRATEFUL FOR:

1. _____

2. _____

3. _____

4. _____

5. _____

6. _____

7. _____

8. _____

9. _____

10. _____

THANK YOU, THANK YOU, THANK YOU!

" It's better to lose count while naming your blessings, than to lose your mind while counting your troubles."

- MALTBIE D. BABCOCK

Date: _____

TODAY, I AM TRULY GRATEFUL FOR:

1. _____

2. _____

3. _____

4. _____

5. _____

6. _____

7. _____

8. _____

9. _____

10. _____

THANK YOU, THANK YOU, THANK YOU!

"Gratitude is the fairest blossom which springs from the soul." — HENRY WARD BEECHER

 Magic Rock Reminder

Date: _____

TODAY, I AM TRULY GRATEFUL FOR:

1. _____

2. _____

3. _____

4. _____

5. _____

6. _____

7. _____

8. _____

9. _____

10. _____

THANK YOU, THANK YOU, THANK YOU!

" ou should set goals beyond your reach so you always ha e something to li e for."

- TED TURNER

Thank You. ....

1.

2.

3.

4.

5.

DAY 3

THANK YOU. ....

1. _____

_____

2. _____

_____

3. _____

_____

4. _____

_____

5. _____

_____

ATTACH A PHOTO HERE

THANK YOU. ....

1.

2.

3.

4.

5.

THE GIFT OF HEALTH IS KEEPING ME ALIVE

Date: _____

TODAY. I AM TRULY GRATEFUL FOR:

1. _____

2. _____

3. _____

4. _____

5. _____

6. _____

7. _____

8. _____

9. _____

10. _____

Thank You. Thank You. Thank You!

"It's better to lose count while naming your blessings, than to lose your mind while counting your troubles!"

– REV RUN SIMMONS

Date: _____

TODAY, I AM TRULY GRATEFUL FOR:

1. _____

2. _____

3. _____

4. _____

5. _____

6. _____

7. _____

8. _____

9. _____

10. _____

THANK YOU, THANK YOU, THANK YOU!

"The more grateful I am, the more beauty I see."

- MARY DAVIS

Date: _____

TODAY, I AM TRULY GRATEFUL FOR:

1. _____

2. _____

3. _____

4. _____

5. _____

6. _____

7. _____

8. _____

9. _____

10. _____

THANK YOU, THANK YOU, THANK YOU!

"When you are grateful, fear disappears and abundance appears."

- ANTHONY ROBBINS

TODAY, I AM TRULY GRATEFUL FOR:

1. _____

2. _____

3. _____

4. _____

5. _____

6. _____

7. _____

8. _____

9. _____

10. _____

THANK YOU, THANK YOU, THANK YOU!

"Gratitude is a powerful catalyst for happiness. It's the spark that lights a fire of joy in your soul."

– AMY COLLETTE

Magically Turn Your Situation Around

....

1. _____

2. _____

3. _____

4. _____

5. _____

6. _____

7. _____

8. _____

9. _____

10. _____

Thank You. Thank You. Thank You. For The Perfect Resolution.

Date: _____

TODAY, I AM TRULY GRATEFUL FOR:

1. _____

2. _____

3. _____

4. _____

5. _____

6. _____

7. _____

8. _____

9. _____

10. _____

Thank You, Thank You, Thank You!

"No duty is more urgent than gi ing thanks."

- ANTHONY ROBBINS

Date: _____

TODAY, I AM TRULY GRATEFUL FOR:

1. _____

2. _____

3. _____

4. _____

5. _____

6. _____

7. _____

8. _____

9. _____

10. _____

THANK YOU. THANK YOU. THANK YOU!

"When it comes to life the critical thing is whether you take things for granted or take them with gratitude."

— G.K. CHESTERTON

Date: _____

TODAY, I AM TRULY GRATEFUL FOR:

1. _____

2. _____

3. _____

4. _____

5. _____

6. _____

7. _____

8. _____

9. _____

10. _____

Thank You. Thank You. Thank You!

"Enjoy the little things, for one day you may look back and realize they were the big things."

– ROBERT BRAULT

　　　　　　　　　Date: _____

TODAY. I AM TRULY GRATEFUL FOR:

1. _____

2. _____

3. _____

4. _____

5. _____

6. _____

7. _____

8. _____

9. _____

10. _____

THANK YOU. THANK YOU. THANK YOU!

"When you arise in the morning, think of what a precious pri ilege it is to be ali e-to breathe, to think, to enjoy, to lo e."

- MARCUS AURELIUS

Date: _____

TODAY, I AM TRULY GRATEFUL FOR:

1. _____

2. _____

3. _____

4. _____

5. _____

6. _____

7. _____

8. _____

9. _____

10. _____

THANK YOU, THANK YOU, THANK YOU!

"If the only prayer you said was thank you, that would be enough."

— MEISTER ECKHART

MAGICAL PEOPLE IN MY LIFE:

....

_____

_____

_____

_____

_____

_____

_____

_____

_____

_____

....

_____

_____

_____

_____

_____

_____

_____

_____

_____

_____

MAGICAL PEOPLE IN MY LIFE:

....

_____

_____

_____

_____

_____

_____

_____

_____

_____

_____

"We must find time to stop and thank the people who make a difference in our li es."

—JOHN F. KENNEDY

Date: _____

TODAY, I AM TRULY GRATEFUL FOR:

1. _____

2. _____

3. _____

4. _____

5. _____

6. _____

7. _____

8. _____

9. _____

10. _____

THANK YOU, THANK YOU, THANK YOU!

"Gratitude is not only the greatest of virtues, but the parent of all others."

— MARCUS TULLIUS CICERO

Top Ten Desires:

1. Thank you. thank you thank you for

2.

3.

4.

5.

6.

7.

8.

9.

10.

"Change your expectation for appreciation and the world changes instantly."

- TONY ROBBINS

TODAY, I AM TRULY GRATEFUL FOR:

1. _____

2. _____

3. _____

4. _____

5. _____

6. _____

7. _____

8. _____

9. _____

10. _____

THANK YOU, THANK YOU, THANK YOU!

"The unthankful heart discovers no mercies; but the thankful heart will find, in every hour, some heavenly blessings."

- HENRY WARD BEECHER

Date: _____

TODAY, I AM TRULY GRATEFUL FOR:

1. _____

2. _____

3. _____

4. _____

5. _____

6. _____

7. _____

8. _____

9. _____

10. _____

THANK YOU. THANK YOU. THANK YOU!

*"The soul that gives thanks can find comfort in everything;
the soul that complains can find comfort in nothing."*

- HANNAH WHITALL SMITH

Ten Things I Am Grateful For About

. . . .

1. _____ . I'm Grateful for _____

_____

2. _____

_____

3. _____

_____

4. _____

_____

5. _____

_____

6. _____

_____

7. _____

_____

8. _____

_____

9. _____

_____

10. _____

_____

"I have found that worry and irritation vanish the moment when I open my mind to the many blessing that I possess."

- DALE CARNEGIE

Date: _____

TODAY, I AM TRULY GRATEFUL FOR:

1. _____

2. _____

3. _____

4. _____

5. _____

6. _____

7. _____

8. _____

9. _____

10. _____

THANK YOU, THANK YOU, THANK YOU!

"When gratitude becomes an essential foundation in our li es, miracles start to appear e erywhere."

– EMMANUEL DAGHER

Date: _____

TODAY, I AM TRULY GRATEFUL FOR:

1. _____

2. _____

3. _____

4. _____

5. _____

6. _____

7. _____

8. _____

9. _____

10. _____

THANK YOU, THANK YOU, THANK YOU!

"Gratitude is riches. Complaint is po erty."

- DORIS DAY

Date: _____

TODAY, I AM TRULY GRATEFUL FOR:

1. _____

2. _____

3. _____

4. _____

5. _____

6. _____

7. _____

8. _____

9. _____

10. _____

THANK YOU, THANK YOU, THANK YOU!

"It is only with gratitude that life becomes rich."

— DIETRICH BONHOEFFER

THE MAGICAL TO- DO LIST

1. _____

2. _____

3. _____

4. _____

5. _____

6. _____

7. _____

8. _____

9. _____

10. _____

" The uni erse is full of magical things, patiently waiting for our wits to grow sharper."

— EDEN PHILLPOTTS

DAY 19

Date: _____

TODAY, I AM TRULY GRATEFUL FOR:

1. _____

2. _____

3. _____

4. _____

5. _____

6. _____

7. _____

8. _____

9. _____

10. _____

THANK YOU, THANK YOU, THANK YOU!

"Be content with what you have; rejoice in the way things are. When you realize there is nothing lacking, the whole world belongs to you."

- LAO TZU

Date: _____

TODAY, I AM TRULY GRATEFUL FOR:

1. _____

2. _____

3. _____

4. _____

5. _____

6. _____

7. _____

8. _____

9. _____

10. _____

THANK YOU, THANK YOU, THANK YOU!

"A thankful heart hath a continual feast."

– W.J. CAMERON

Date: _____

TODAY, I AM TRULY GRATEFUL FOR:

1. _____

2. _____

3. _____

4. _____

5. _____

6. _____

7. _____

8. _____

9. _____

10. _____

THANK YOU, THANK YOU, THANK YOU!

"Acknowledging the good that you already have in your life is the foundation for all abundance."

– ECKHART TOLLE

Magnificent Outcomes

1. Thank You For The Magnificent Outcome To

2.

3.

Notes

_____
_____
_____
_____
_____
_____
_____
_____
_____
_____

"If you concentrate on finding whate er is good in e ery situation, you will disco er that your life will suddenly be filled with gratitude, a feeling that nurtures the soul."

— RABBI HAROLD KUSHNER

TODAY, I AM TRULY GRATEFUL FOR:

1. _____

2. _____

3. _____

4. _____

5. _____

6. _____

7. _____

8. _____

9. _____

10. _____

THANK YOU, THANK YOU, THANK YOU!

"A grateful mind is a great mind which eventually attracts to itself great things."

– PLATO

Top Ten Desire List:

1. _____

2. _____

3. _____

4. _____

5. _____

6. _____

7. _____

8. _____

9. _____

10. _____

"When we gi e cheerfully and accept gratefully, e eryone is blessed."

– MAYA ANGELOU

Top Ten Desire List:

1. _____

2. _____

3. _____

4. _____

5. _____

6. _____

7. _____

8. _____

9. _____

10. _____

"When we gi e cheerfully and accept gratefully,
e eryone is blessed."

– MAYA ANGELOU

DAY 23

Date: _____

TODAY. I AM TRULY GRATEFUL FOR:

1. _____

2. _____

3. _____

4. _____

5. _____

6. _____

7. _____

8. _____

9. _____

10. _____

THANK YOU. THANK YOU. THANK YOU!

"There is a calmness to a life lived in gratitude, a quiet joy."

- RALPH H. BLUM

Date: _____

TODAY, I AM TRULY GRATEFUL FOR:

1. _____

2. _____

3. _____

4. _____

5. _____

6. _____

7. _____

8. _____

9. _____

10. _____

THANK YOU, THANK YOU, THANK YOU!

"Blessed are they who see beautiful things in humble places where other people see nothing."

- CAMILLE PISSARRO

Date: _____

TODAY, I AM TRULY GRATEFUL FOR:

1. _____

2. _____

3. _____

4. _____

5. _____

6. _____

7. _____

8. _____

9. _____

10. _____

THANK YOU, THANK YOU, THANK YOU!

*"God ga e you a gift of 84,600 seconds today.
Ha e you used one of them to say thank you?"*

– WILLIAM ARTHUR WARD

MAGICALLY TRANSFORM MISTAKES INTO BESSINGS

WHAT DID I LEARN FROM THE MISTAKE?

1. _____

_____

_____

2. _____

_____

_____

3. _____

_____

_____

4. _____

_____

_____

5. _____

_____

_____

"Some people grumble that roses ha e thorns; I am grateful that thorns ha e roses."

- ALPHONSE KARR

Magically Transform Mistakes Into Bessings

What are the good things that came out of the mistake?

6. _____
_____
_____

7. _____
_____
_____
_____

8. _____
_____
_____

9. _____
_____
_____

10. _____
_____
_____
_____

"As with all commandments, gratitude is a description of a successful mode of li ing. The thankful heart opens our eyes to a multitude of blessings that continually surround us."

- JAMES E. FAUST

Date: _____

TODAY, I AM TRULY GRATEFUL FOR:

1. _____

2. _____

3. _____

4. _____

5. _____

6. _____

7. _____

8. _____

9. _____

10. _____

THANK YOU. THANK YOU. THANK YOU!

"I don't ha e to chase extraordinary moments to find happiness – it's right in front of me if I'm paying attention and practicing gratitude."

- BRENE BROWN

Date: _____

TODAY. I AM TRULY GRATEFUL FOR:

1. _____

2. _____

3. _____

4. _____

5. _____

6. _____

7. _____

8. _____

9. _____

10. _____

THANK YOU. THANK YOU. THANK YOU!

"Learn to be thankful for what you already have, while you pursue all that you want."

- JIM ROHN

Date: _____

TODAY, I AM TRULY GRATEFUL FOR:

1. _____

2. _____

3. _____

4. _____

5. _____

6. _____

7. _____

8. _____

9. _____

10. _____

THANK YOU. THANK YOU. THANK YOU!

"Appreciation can make a day, e en change a life. our willingness to put it into words is all that is necessary."

- MARGARET COUSINS

Counting Yesterday's Blessings

What are the good things that happened yesterday?

1.

2.

3.

4.

5.

6.

7.

8.

9.

10.

"Gratitude goes beyond the 'mine' and 'thine' and claims the truth that all of life is a pure gift."

— HENRI J.M. NOUWEN

Affirm Your Way to Success: A Guide to Using Affirmations in Your Magic Journal

Introduction:
Affirm Your Way to Success is a guide to using affirmations to enhance your journey of gratitude and manifestation with Your Magic Journal. Affirmations are positive statements that you repeat to yourself to boost your self-confidence and improve your overall well-being. In this short guide, we will explore the benefits of using affirmations and how you can incorporate them into your daily gratitude practice with Your Magic Journal.

Explanation:
To get the most out of your affirmations, it's important to understand the power of positive self-talk. Your thoughts and beliefs have a profound impact on your emotions, behaviors, and overall life experiences. By repeating positive affirmations, you can train your mind to focus on the positive and overcome negative thoughts and beliefs.

Here's how to use affirmations in Your Magic Journal:

*1. **Choose affirmations that resonate with you:** Choose affirmations that align with your goals and aspirations. You can use the 120 affirmations provided in this guide or come up with your own.*

*2. **Write them down:** Write down your affirmations in Your Magic Journal and refer to them often. Seeing the affirmations written down reinforces their power and impact.*

*3. **Repeat them daily:** Repeat your affirmations daily, either out loud or silently to yourself. Repeat each affirmation multiple times and feel the positive energy that it brings.*

*4. **Visualize them:** Close your eyes and visualize yourself living out each affirmation. See yourself happy, successful, and fulfilled.*

*5. **Track your progress:** Keep track of your progress and the changes you see in yourself. Seeing positive changes will further reinforce the power of your affirmations.*

Incorporating affirmations into your daily gratitude practice with Your Magic Journal will amplify the positive impact that you see in your life. So start affirming your way to success today!

1. *I am worthy of love and happiness.*
2. *I am deserving of success and abundance.*
3. *I am grateful for all the blessings in my life.*
4. *I am confident and strong.*
5. *I attract positivity and abundance into my life.*
6. *I am capable of achieving my goals.*
7. *I am surrounded by love and support.*
8. *I am filled with joy and happiness.*
9. *I trust the universe to guide me on my path.*
10. *I choose to focus on the positive in every situation.*
11. *I am at peace with myself and my life.*
12. *I am grateful for every experience, good and bad.*
13. *I am constantly improving and growing.*
14. *I am surrounded by beauty and abundance.*
15. *I am deserving of love and respect.*
16. *I am confident in my abilities and decisions.*
17. *I am grateful for my strengths and abilities.*
18. *I am surrounded by abundance and prosperity.*
19. *I am in control of my thoughts and emotions.*
20. *I choose to live in the present moment.*
21. *I am grateful for my health and well-being.*
22. *I am worthy of success in all areas of my life.*
23. *I am surrounded by positivity and good energy.*
24. *I am confident in my ability to achieve my dreams.*
25. *I am grateful for my relationships and connections with others.*
26. *I am open to new opportunities and experiences.*
27. *I am at peace with my past and focused on my future.*
28. *I am grateful for my experiences and lessons learned.*
29. *I am worthy of love and acceptance.*
30. *I am surrounded by abundance and success.*

31. *I choose to focus on my blessings, not my struggles.*

32. *I am grateful for my resilience and determination.*

33. *I am confident in my ability to overcome challenges.*

34. *I am surrounded by joy and happiness.*

35. *I am worthy of financial abundance.*

36. *I am grateful for my talents and abilities.*

37. *I am open to receiving abundance in all forms.*

38. *I am at peace with myself and my life journey.*

39. *I am grateful for my growth and progress.*

40. *I am worthy of love and support.*

41. *I am surrounded by positivity and good vibes.*

42. *I am confident in my ability to achieve my goals.*

43. *I am grateful for my journey and the person I am becoming.*

44. *I am open to new experiences and opportunities.*

45. *I am at peace with my past and focused on my future.*

46. *I am grateful for my inner peace and stability.*

47. *I am worthy of financial stability and success.*

48. *I am surrounded by abundance and prosperity.*

49. *I choose to focus on the positive in every situation.*

50. *I am grateful for my progress and accomplishments.*

51. *I am confident in my ability to overcome obstacles.*

52. *I am surrounded by love and light.*

53. *I am worthy of happiness and contentment.*

54. *I am grateful for my courage and bravery.*

55. *I am open to receiving abundance in all areas of my life.*

56. *I am at peace with my journey and where it leads me.*

57. *I am grateful for my growth and transformation.*

58. *I am worthy of success and recognition.*

59. *I am surrounded by positivity and success.*

60. *I am deserving of love, joy, and abundance in all areas of my life.*

61. I am grateful for my determination and motivation.

62. I am confident in my ability to make a positive impact on the world.

63. I am surrounded by peace and tranquility.

64. I am worthy of love and appreciation.

65. I am grateful for my ability to learn and grow.

66. I am open to new perspectives and ideas.

67. I am at peace with who I am and where I am in life.

68. I am grateful for my inner strength and wisdom.

69. I am worthy of financial freedom and security.

70. I am surrounded by positive energy and good karma.

71. I choose to focus on my blessings and be thankful.

72. I am grateful for my creativity and originality.

73. I am confident in my ability to overcome fear and doubt.

74. I am surrounded by love and understanding.

75. I am worthy of respect and kindness.

76. I am grateful for my compassion and empathy.

77. I am open to receiving love and support.

78. I am at peace with my journey and the person I am becoming.

79. I am grateful for my courage to pursue my passions.

80. I am worthy of abundance and prosperity.

81. I am surrounded by good luck and fortune.

82. I choose to focus on the present moment and live life to the fullest.

83. I am grateful for my ability to heal and recover.

84. I am confident in my ability to make a positive change in my life.

85. I am surrounded by beauty and inspiration.

86. I am worthy of love and acceptance for who I am.

87. I am grateful for my inner peace and happiness.

88. I am open to new adventures and challenges.

89. I am at peace with the ups and downs of life.

90. I am grateful for my ability to adapt and evolve.

91. I am worthy of financial stability and success.

92. I am surrounded by positivity and prosperity.

93. I choose to focus on my progress, not my failures.

94. I am grateful for my determination and resilience.

95. I am confident in my ability to make a difference in the world.

96. I am surrounded by love and positivity.

97. I am worthy of happiness and fulfillment.

98. I am grateful for my passions and interests.

99. I am open to new opportunities and experiences.

100. I am grateful for all that I have and all that is yet to come.

101. I am filled with confidence and strength.

102. I am capable of achieving my greatest dreams.

103. I am in control of my thoughts and emotions.

104. I am surrounded by positive and supportive people.

105. I choose to see the good in every situation.

106. I am grateful for my many blessings.

107. I am worthy of success and abundance.

108. I am strong, resilient, and capable.

109. I attract abundance and prosperity into my life.

110. I am filled with joy and happiness.

111. I am confident and optimistic about the future.

112. I choose to focus on the positive in all aspects of my life.

113. I am worthy of love, respect, and happiness.

114. I am grateful for my body and all that it allows me to do.

115. I am deserving of success and abundance in all areas of my life.

116. I am capable of overcoming any obstacle that comes my way.

117. I am confident in my abilities and trust in my journey.

118. I am surrounded by positivity, love, and light.

119. I am deserving of abundance and happiness.

120. I trust the universe to guide me toward my greatest happiness.

Visualization Exercises for Gratitude and Manifestation

Introduction:
Visualization is a powerful tool in manifestation and personal growth. By using your imagination to focus on your desired outcomes, you can bring your goals and aspirations closer to reality. In this chapter, we will explore several visualization exercises that can enhance your gratitude practice and bring you closer to your desired outcomes.

Exercise 1: Imagine Your Desired Outcome

In "The Magic" Rhonda encourages readers to imagine their desired outcome as a way of manifesting their goals and desires. This exercise involves using visualization and positive affirmations to bring your desires to life in your mind and align your thoughts and actions with your goals. Here's how to do this exercise properly:

1. Get clear on your desired outcome: Take some time to think about what you truly want to manifest in your life. Whether it's a specific goal, a new job, a loving relationship, or a greater sense of happiness, get clear on what you want to achieve.
2. Create a vivid visual image: Close your eyes and imagine your desired outcome as vividly as possible. Use all of your senses to bring the image to life in your mind. See yourself achieving your goal, feel the emotions that come with it, and hear the sounds and experiences associated with it.
3. Repeat positive affirmations: As you visualize your desired outcome, repeat positive affirmations that align with your goal. For example, if you're imagining a new job, you might say something like "I am confident and capable, and I easily attract the perfect job for me." Repeat these affirmations several times, and focus on the feelings of excitement and confidence they bring.
4. Focus on the positive: As you visualize and repeat your affirmations, focus on the positive aspects of your desired outcome. Imagine yourself experiencing success, joy, and abundance, and let go of any negative thoughts or doubts.
5. Make it a daily habit: Make imagining your desired outcome a daily habit, and spend time each day visualizing and affirming your goal. The more you focus on your desired outcome, the more likely you are to manifest it in your life.
6. Take inspired action: While visualization and affirmations are powerful tools for manifesting your desires, it's important to also take inspired action towards your goal. Trust your intuition and take steps towards your desired outcome, and trust that the universe is working in your favor to bring your goal to life.

This exercise can help you align your thoughts and actions with your desired outcome, and it can also help you cultivate gratitude by focusing on the positive aspects of your life and what you're grateful for. Whether you're just starting out or you're looking to deepen your practice, imagining your desired outcome can be a valuable tool for manifesting your goals and living a life filled with abundance and joy.

Exercise 2: Create a Vision Board
A vision board is a visual representation of your goals, dreams, and desires. By creating a vision board, you can bring your desires to life in a tangible and inspiring way, and use it as a daily reminder of what you're working towards. Here's how to create a vision board:

1. Gather materials: You'll need a large poster board, magazines, scissors, glue, and any other decorative items you'd like to use.
2. Get clear on your goals: Take some time to think about what you want to manifest in your life. Consider your career, relationships, health, and personal growth, and identify the specific goals and desires you want to focus on.
3. Cut out images and words: Go through magazines and cut out images and words that represent your goals and desires. These could be pictures of people, places, or things you'd like to manifest, or words that describe how you want to feel.
4. Arrange your images and words: Arrange the images and words on your poster board, and play around with different arrangements until you find one that resonates with you.
5. Add any additional elements: Use glue to secure the images and words to the poster board, and add any additional elements you'd like, such as stickers, washi tape, or other decorative items.
6. Place your vision board in a visible location: Hang your vision board in a location where you'll see it regularly, such as on your bedroom wall or near your workspace.
7. Review your vision board regularly: Take time each day to review your vision board, and focus on the goals and desires you've included. Use your vision board as a daily reminder of what you're working towards, and let it inspire you to take action towards your goals.

Creating a vision board can help you bring your desires to life and keep them top of mind, and it can also help you cultivate gratitude by focusing on what you're grateful for and what you're working towards. Whether you're just starting out or you're looking to deepen your practice, a vision board can be a valuable tool for manifesting your goals and living a life filled with abundance and joy.

Exercise 3: Write a Detailed Description

Writing a detailed description of your goals and desires can help you bring them to life in your mind and align your thoughts and actions with your goals. This exercise involves taking the time to write out a clear and detailed description of what you want to manifest in your life. Here's how to do this exercise:

1. *Get clear on your goals: Take some time to think about what you want to manifest in your life. Consider your career, relationships, health, and personal growth, and identify the specific goals and desires you want to focus on.*
2. *Write a detailed description: Using a notebook or a word processing program on your computer, write a detailed description of your goals and desires. Be as specific and vivid as possible, and include as many details as you can. Use all of your senses to bring your goals to life in your mind, and imagine yourself experiencing success, joy, and abundance.*
3. *Focus on the positive: As you write, focus on the positive aspects of your desired outcome, and let go of any negative thoughts or doubts. Write as if your goals and desires have already been manifested, and use positive language and affirmations to reinforce your positive outlook.*
4. *Review your description regularly: Take time each day to review your description, and focus on the goals and desires you've included. Use your description as a daily reminder of what you're working towards, and let it inspire you to take action towards your goals.*
5. *Update your description as needed: As you work towards your goals, you may find that your desires and priorities change. Update your description as needed to reflect these changes, and keep your focus on what you're working towards.*

Writing a detailed description of your goals and desires can help you bring them to life in your mind and align your thoughts and actions with your goals. By taking the time to write out a clear and vivid description, you can deepen your practice of gratitude and experience the many benefits it brings. Whether you're just starting out or you're looking to deepen your practice, writing a detailed description can be a valuable tool for manifesting your goals and living a life filled with abundance and joy.

Use the space on the next pages of Your Magic Journal to do this exercise. This will give you a dedicated space to write out your goals and desires, and you can refer back to your description whenever you need inspiration or motivation.

Exercise 4: Visualize a White Light

Visualizing a white light is a powerful way to bring a sense of calm and well-being to your life. This exercise involves imagining a bright white light surrounding you, filling you with positive energy and protection. Here's how to do this exercise:

1. Find a quiet space: Find a quiet and comfortable place where you can sit or lie down without distractions. Turn off your phone and other devices, and close your eyes if you like.
2. Take a deep breath: Begin by taking a few deep breaths, inhaling deeply through your nose and exhaling slowly through your mouth. This can help you relax and focus your mind.
3. Visualize a white light: Imagine a bright white light surrounding you, starting from your feet and rising up to your head. See the light filling your body and surrounding you, bringing you a sense of peace and well-being.
4. Focus on the light: Focus your attention on the white light, and imagine it filling you with positive energy and protection. See the light shining brightly, and feel its warmth and comfort.
5. Repeat positive affirmations: As you focus on the white light, repeat positive affirmations that align with your goals and desires. For example, you might say something like "I am surrounded by love and light, and I am protected and safe." Repeat these affirmations several times, and focus on the feelings of peace and comfort they bring.
6. Take a few more deep breaths: When you're ready, take a few more deep breaths, and imagine the white light either fading away or continuing to surround and protect you. Choose what resonates with you more and helps you process better. Visualizing the light fading away can symbolize letting go of stress and negative thoughts while imagining it surrounding you can symbolize feeling protected and safe. The goal is to bring peace and well-being and to cultivate gratitude.

Visualizing a white light can help you bring a sense of calm and well-being to your life, and it can also help you cultivate gratitude by focusing on the positive aspects of your life and what you're grateful for.

Exercise 5: Create a gratitude jar or box

A gratitude jar or box is a simple but powerful tool for cultivating gratitude in your life. This exercise involves creating a physical container where you can collect and store items that represent the things you're grateful for. Here's how to create a gratitude jar or box:

1. Gather materials: You'll need a jar or box, paper, and a pen or marker. You can decorate your jar or box however you like, using paint, stickers, or other decorative elements.

2. *Write down what you're grateful for:* Each day, take a moment to write down something you're grateful for on a slip of paper. This could be something as small as a warm meal, a kind word from a friend, or a beautiful sunset.
3. *Store your gratitude slips:* Fold each slip of paper and place it in your gratitude jar or box. You can store your gratitude slips for as long or as little as you like, and you can revisit them whenever you need a boost of positivity.
4. *Celebrate your blessings:* Over time, your gratitude jar or box will fill up with reminders of the many blessings in your life. Take time each day to reflect on what you're grateful for, and celebrate the good things in your life.
5. *Share your gratitude with others:* You can also share your gratitude with others by sharing your gratitude slips or by encouraging others to create their own gratitude jars or boxes.

Creating a gratitude jar or box can help you cultivate gratitude in your life, and it can also serve as a visual reminder of the many blessings in your life. Whether you're just starting out or you're looking to deepen your practice, a gratitude jar or box can be a valuable tool for living a life filled with abundance and joy.

Exercise 6: Practice a manifestation ritual
Practicing a manifestation ritual is a powerful way to bring your goals and desires to life. This exercise involves incorporating specific actions and affirmations into your daily routine to help you align your thoughts and actions with your goals. Here's how to practice a manifestation ritual:
1. *Get clear on your goals:* Take some time to think about what you want to manifest in your life. Consider your career, relationships, health, and personal growth, and identify the specific goals and desires you want to focus on.
2. *Choose a manifestation ritual:* Choose a manifestation ritual that resonates with you, such as visualization, affirmations, or writing a detailed description of your goals.
3. *Practice at powerful times:* The most powerful times to practice your manifestation ritual are when you are connected to your right brain hemisphere, such as right before going to sleep, after waking up, and after meditation.
4. *Focus on the positive:* As you practice your manifestation ritual, focus on the positive aspects of your desired outcome, and let go of any negative thoughts or doubts. See yourself experiencing success, joy, and abundance, and use positive affirmations to reinforce your positive outlook.
5. *Make it a daily habit:* Make your manifestation ritual a daily habit, and practice it at the same time each day. The more you focus on

your goals and desires, the more likely you are to manifest them in your life.

6. *Take inspired action: While your manifestation ritual is an important part of bringing your goals to life, it's also important to take inspired action towards your goals. Trust your intuition, and take steps towards your desired outcome, knowing that the universe is working in your favor to bring your goal to life.*

Practicing a manifestation ritual can help you align your thoughts and actions with your goals, and it can also help you cultivate gratitude by focusing on the positive aspects of your life and what you're grateful for.

Congratulations on reaching the end of this magic journal!

By following the exercises and practices outlined in this journal, you've taken an important step towards manifesting your goals and desires and living a life filled with abundance and joy.

The power of gratitude is truly transformative, and by incorporating it into your daily life, you can experience its many benefits. Whether you're just starting out or you're looking to deepen your practice, the exercises and practices in this journal can help you cultivate gratitude, align your thoughts and actions with your goals, and bring your desires to life.

Remember that manifestation is a journey, not a destination. Trust the process, and trust that the universe is working in your favor to bring your goals to life. Keep focusing on the positive aspects of your life, and let go of any negative thoughts or doubts. And most importantly, never stop believing in yourself and your ability to manifest your dreams.

Thank yourself for committing to this journey and for taking the time to focus on gratitude and manifestation. The power of gratitude is truly transformative, and by incorporating it into your daily life, you can experience its many benefits.

To continue your journey towards manifestation and gratitude, remember to "Remember the Magic" by incorporating these practices into your daily life and focusing on gratitude every day. To aid in this, we have included additional pages in this journal for you to practice gratitude for the next 30 days. Write down what you're grateful for each day to keep your focus on gratitude and serve as a visual reminder of the blessings in your life. By practicing gratitude and incorporating these exercises, you'll deepen your connection to the magic within you and experience the benefits of a grateful heart. Keep up the great work and always remember that the magic is within reach.

REMEMBER THE MAGIC

TODAY, I AM TRULY GRATEFUL FOR:

1. _____

2. _____

3. _____

4. _____

5. _____

6. _____

7. _____

8. _____

9. _____

10. _____

THANK YOU. THANK YOU. THANK YOU!

Date: _____

TODAY, I AM TRULY GRATEFUL FOR:

1. _____

2. _____

3. _____

4. _____

5. _____

6. _____

7. _____

8. _____

9. _____

10. _____

THANK YOU. THANK YOU. THANK YOU!

TODAY, I AM TRULY GRATEFUL FOR:

1. _____

2. _____

3. _____

4. _____

5. _____

6. _____

7. _____

8. _____

9. _____

10. _____

THANK YOU, THANK YOU, THANK YOU!

TODAY, I AM TRULY GRATEFUL FOR:

1. _____

2. _____

3. _____

4. _____

5. _____

6. _____

7. _____

8. _____

9. _____

10. _____

THANK YOU, THANK YOU, THANK YOU!

TODAY, I AM TRULY GRATEFUL FOR:

1. _____

2. _____

3. _____

4. _____

5. _____

6. _____

7. _____

8. _____

9. _____

10. _____

THANK YOU, THANK YOU, THANK YOU!

TODAY. I AM TRULY GRATEFUL FOR:

1. _____

2. _____

3. _____

4. _____

5. _____

6. _____

7. _____

8. _____

9. _____

10. _____

THANK YOU. THANK YOU. THANK YOU!

TODAY, I AM TRULY GRATEFUL FOR:

1. _____

2. _____

3. _____

4. _____

5. _____

6. _____

7. _____

8. _____

9. _____

10. _____

THANK YOU, THANK YOU, THANK YOU!

Date: _____

TODAY. I AM TRULY GRATEFUL FOR:

1. _____

2. _____

3. _____

4. _____

5. _____

6. _____

7. _____

8. _____

9. _____

10. _____

THANK YOU. THANK YOU. THANK YOU!

TODAY, I AM TRULY GRATEFUL FOR:

1. _____

2. _____

3. _____

4. _____

5. _____

6. _____

7. _____

8. _____

9. _____

10. _____

THANK YOU, THANK YOU, THANK YOU!

Date: _____

TODAY, I AM TRULY GRATEFUL FOR:

1. _____

2. _____

3. _____

4. _____

5. _____

6. _____

7. _____

8. _____

9. _____

10. _____

THANK YOU, THANK YOU, THANK YOU!

Date: _____

TODAY, I AM TRULY GRATEFUL FOR:

1. _____

2. _____

3. _____

4. _____

5. _____

6. _____

7. _____

8. _____

9. _____

10. _____

THANK YOU, THANK YOU, THANK YOU!

Date: _____

TODAY, I AM TRULY GRATEFUL FOR:

1. _____

_____

2. _____

_____

3. _____

_____

4. _____

_____

5. _____

_____

6. _____

_____

7. _____

_____

8. _____

_____

9. _____

_____

10. _____

_____

THANK YOU, THANK YOU, THANK YOU!

TODAY, I AM TRULY GRATEFUL FOR:

1. _____

2. _____

3. _____

4. _____

5. _____

6. _____

7. _____

8. _____

9. _____

10. _____

THANK YOU, THANK YOU, THANK YOU!

TODAY. I AM TRULY GRATEFUL FOR:

1. _____

2. _____

3. _____

4. _____

5. _____

6. _____

7. _____

8. _____

9. _____

10. _____

THANK YOU. THANK YOU. THANK YOU!

TODAY, I AM TRULY GRATEFUL FOR:

1. _____

2. _____

3. _____

4. _____

5. _____

6. _____

7. _____

8. _____

9. _____

10. _____

THANK YOU, THANK YOU, THANK YOU!

Date: _____

TODAY, I AM TRULY GRATEFUL FOR:

1. _____

2. _____

3. _____

4. _____

5. _____

6. _____

7. _____

8. _____

9. _____

10. _____

THANK YOU. THANK YOU. THANK YOU!

TODAY, I AM TRULY GRATEFUL FOR:

1. _____

2. _____

3. _____

4. _____

5. _____

6. _____

7. _____

8. _____

9. _____

10. _____

THANK YOU, THANK YOU, THANK YOU!

TODAY, I AM TRULY GRATEFUL FOR:

1. _____

2. _____

3. _____

4. _____

5. _____

6. _____

7. _____

8. _____

9. _____

10. _____

THANK YOU, THANK YOU, THANK YOU!

TODAY, I AM TRULY GRATEFUL FOR:

1. _____

2. _____

3. _____

4. _____

5. _____

6. _____

7. _____

8. _____

9. _____

10. _____

THANK YOU, THANK YOU, THANK YOU!

Date: _____

TODAY, I AM TRULY GRATEFUL FOR:

1. _____

2. _____

3. _____

4. _____

5. _____

6. _____

7. _____

8. _____

9. _____

10. _____

THANK YOU, THANK YOU, THANK YOU!

Date: _____

TODAY, I AM TRULY GRATEFUL FOR:

1. _____

2. _____

3. _____

4. _____

5. _____

6. _____

7. _____

8. _____

9. _____

10. _____

THANK YOU, THANK YOU, THANK YOU!

TODAY, I AM TRULY GRATEFUL FOR:

1. _____

2. _____

3. _____

4. _____

5. _____

6. _____

7. _____

8. _____

9. _____

10. _____

THANK YOU, THANK YOU, THANK YOU!

TODAY, I AM TRULY GRATEFUL FOR:

1. _____

2. _____

3. _____

4. _____

5. _____

6. _____

7. _____

8. _____

9. _____

10. _____

THANK YOU, THANK YOU, THANK YOU!

Date: _____

TODAY, I AM TRULY GRATEFUL FOR:

1. _____

2. _____

3. _____

4. _____

5. _____

6. _____

7. _____

8. _____

9. _____

10. _____

THANK YOU, THANK YOU, THANK YOU!

TODAY, I AM TRULY GRATEFUL FOR:

1. _____

2. _____

3. _____

4. _____

5. _____

6. _____

7. _____

8. _____

9. _____

10. _____

THANK YOU. THANK YOU. THANK YOU!

Date: _____

TODAY, I AM TRULY GRATEFUL FOR:

1. _____

2. _____

3. _____

4. _____

5. _____

6. _____

7. _____

8. _____

9. _____

10. _____

THANK YOU. THANK YOU. THANK YOU!

TODAY, I AM TRULY GRATEFUL FOR:

1. _____

2. _____

3. _____

4. _____

5. _____

6. _____

7. _____

8. _____

9. _____

10. _____

THANK YOU, THANK YOU, THANK YOU!

Date: _____

TODAY, I AM TRULY GRATEFUL FOR:

1. _____

2. _____

3. _____

4. _____

5. _____

6. _____

7. _____

8. _____

9. _____

10. _____

THANK YOU. THANK YOU. THANK YOU!

Date: _____

TODAY, I AM TRULY GRATEFUL FOR:

1. _____

2. _____

3. _____

4. _____

5. _____

6. _____

7. _____

8. _____

9. _____

10. _____

THANK YOU, THANK YOU, THANK YOU!

TODAY, I AM TRULY GRATEFUL FOR:

1. _____

2. _____

3. _____

4. _____

5. _____

6. _____

7. _____

8. _____

9. _____

10. _____

THANK YOU, THANK YOU, THANK YOU!

I can do Anything

SPACE FOR YOUR REFLECTIONS

SPACE FOR YOUR REFLECTIONS

SPACE FOR YOUR REFLECTIONS

SPACE FOR YOUR REFLECTIONS

Dream
BIG

SPACE FOR YOUR REFLECTIONS

SPACE FOR YOUR REFLECTIONS

SPACE FOR YOUR REFLECTIONS

SPACE FOR YOUR REFLECTIONS

SPACE FOR YOUR REFLECTIONS

_____
_____
_____
_____
_____
_____
_____
_____
_____
_____
_____
_____
_____
_____
_____
_____
_____
_____
_____
_____
_____
_____
_____
_____
_____
_____
_____
_____
_____
_____

SCAN ME

Discover More Products from Belffy Books

www.belffy.com